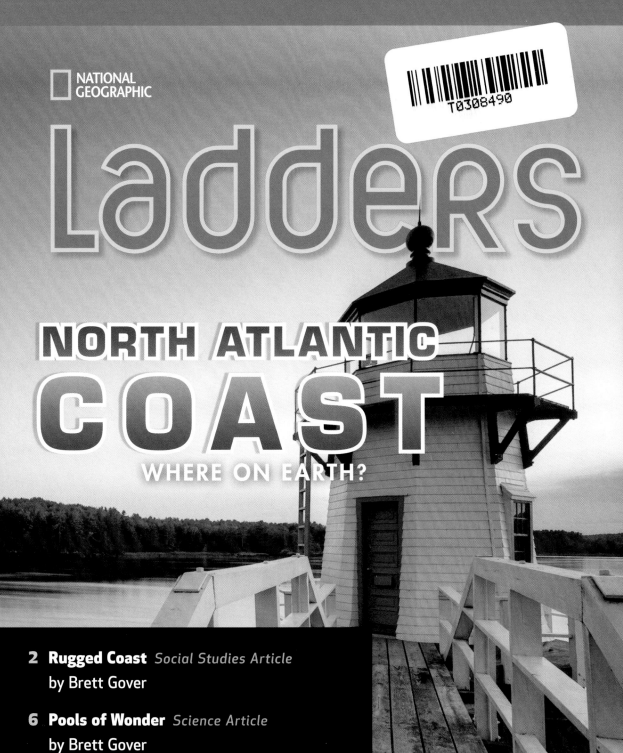

NATIONAL GEOGRAPHIC

Ladders

NORTH ATLANTIC COAST

WHERE ON EARTH?

Read to find out about the geography of the North Atlantic coast.

Rugged Coast

by Brett Gover

Lighthouses help boaters navigate the North Atlantic coast. This lighthouse is in Maine.

Picture a seagull soaring over the North Atlantic coast from Maine to Virginia. What do you suppose the gull sees as it flies south along the coast?

In Maine, at the north end of the region, the gull flies over a rocky and twisting coastline. The ocean seems to cut into the land, forming large bodies of water called **bays** and smaller bodies of water called **coves**. Many islands lie a short distance from the shore, and fishing villages and harbors full of boats line the coast.

Farther south, the coastline becomes straighter and less rocky. Larger towns and cities appear. Leaving Maine, the gull soars south along the edge of New Hampshire and then Massachusetts. It gets a birds-eye view of Boston and the famous outline of Cape Cod. A **cape** is a point of land that sticks out into the ocean.

After following the coasts of Rhode Island and Connecticut, the land juts out into the ocean as the gull passes the towering buildings of New York City. It then flies over New Jersey, Delaware, and Maryland. Soon, the gull is soaring over beach towns, pine forests, and long, narrow islands.

After crossing the wide mouth of Chesapeake (CHESS-uh-peek) Bay, the gull reaches Virginia. The land along the coast, which was hilly farther north, has become very flat. At the end of its long flight, the gull will have traveled about 800 miles along a rugged coast.

Where on Earth?

THE NORTH ATLANTIC COAST

There are lots of cool things to know about the North Atlantic coast. It is home to a wide variety of wildlife, as well as some of the oldest and most important cities in the United States. Here are some facts about the North Atlantic states that might surprise you.

New Hampshire

Several varieties of large whales travel through the waters off the North Atlantic coast. Whale watching tours such as those in New Hampshire give people a chance to see a humpback whale (shown here) up close.

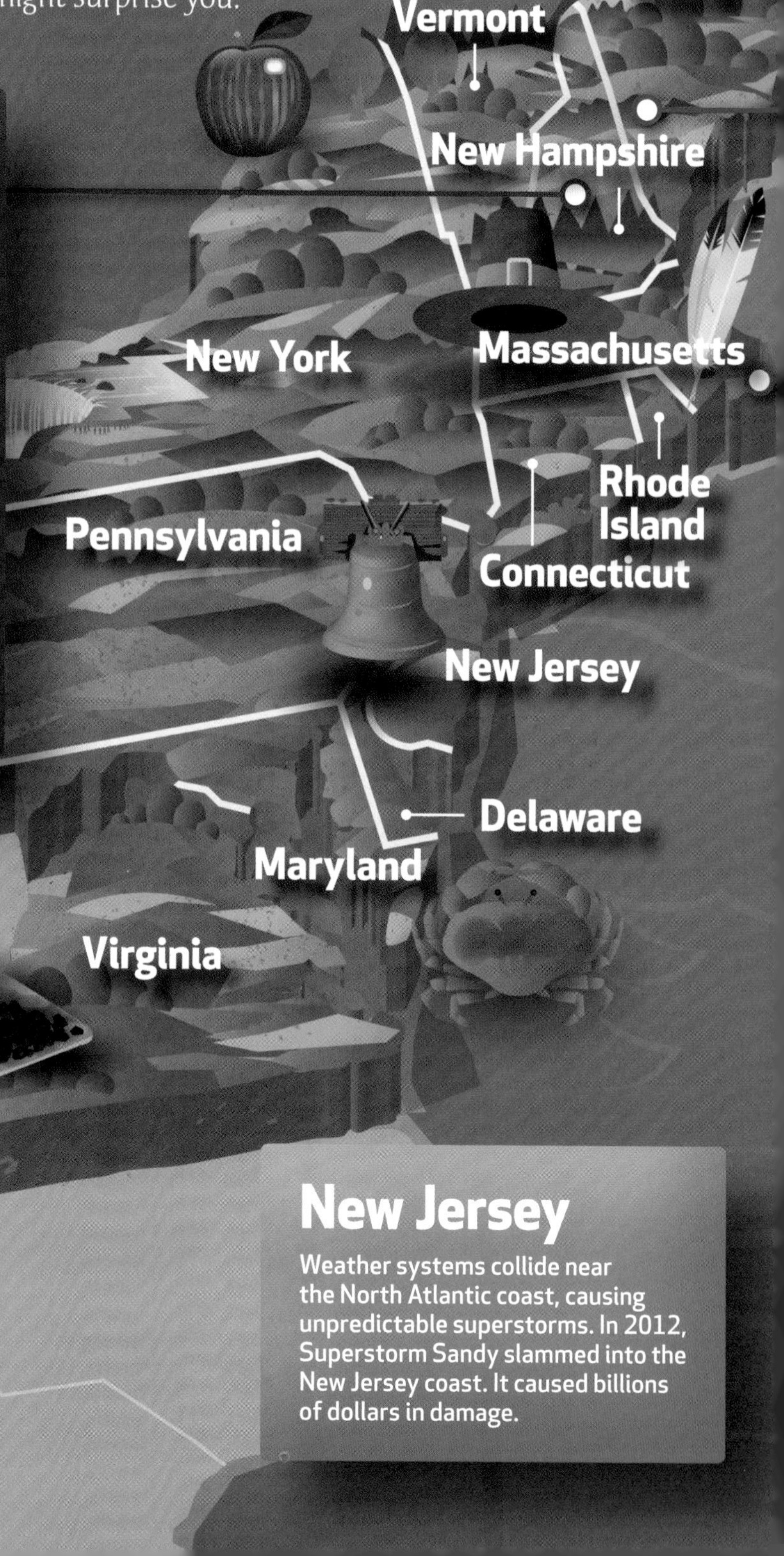

Vermont

Maine

New Hampshire

New York

Massachusetts

Pennsylvania

Rhode Island

Connecticut

New Jersey

Delaware

Maryland

Virginia

New Jersey

Weather systems collide near the North Atlantic coast, causing unpredictable superstorms. In 2012, Superstorm Sandy slammed into the New Jersey coast. It caused billions of dollars in damage.

Maine

In 2012, a lobster weighing 27 pounds was caught off the coast of Maine. The 40-inch-long beast was returned to the ocean. It might still be out there growing larger!

People who live along the northern coast of Maine know that fog can creep up on them at any time. Moose Peak Lighthouse on Mistake Island ranks as the foggiest place on the Atlantic coast.

Massachusetts

Harvard University (above) is the oldest college in the United States.

Boston, Massachusetts, is a city of firsts. The city claims the first lighthouse, first public park, first public school, first college, and first subway in the United States. It was also the first U.S. city to host an annual marathon race.

Rhode Island

Rhode Island is the smallest U.S. state. Roughly 425 states the size of Rhode Island could fit inside Alaska, the largest state.

New York

The area from Boston to Washington, D.C., is a **megalopolis**, a large area of closely connected cities. It stretches more than 400 miles and is home to around one-sixth of the U.S. population. It includes Philadelphia, Baltimore, and New York City (above), the nation's largest city, which is in the state of New York. The Statue of Liberty stands in New York Harbor, welcoming all to the United States.

Check In How does the coastline change throughout the North Atlantic region?

Pools of WOND

by Brett Gover

> These children explore tide pools at Odiorne Point State Park in New Hampshire.

Whoosh!

The loudest sound you'll hear standing on the coast of Maine might be the sound of the water. For creatures that live at the edge of the ocean, there is a rhythm to each day—the rhythm of the **tides**.

Tides are all about gravity. Gravity from both the moon and the sun pulls on Earth. This pull—especially from the moon—causes the ocean level to rise and fall. Here's how: as Earth spins, gravity pulls ocean water high up the shore in some places and away from the shore in others. This causes tides. When it's "high tide" on the coast of Maine, the ocean covers most of the beach. About six hours later, at "low tide," the water stays farther out in the sea. This reveals much more of the rocks and beach.

Animals living in the shallow areas of the ocean also follow this daily schedule. Their homes are completely covered by the ocean during high tide—and then uncovered again as the tide goes out. When the tide goes out along rocky coastlines such as those in northern Maine, it leaves pools of seawater behind called **tide pools**.

Life is not always easy for the creatures that live in these tide pools. High tide sometimes carries large, hungry fish into tide pools. At low tide, the hot sun beats down on tide pool creatures, while hungry birds and other animals come looking for easy snacks on the beach. What will you find in a tide pool? Let's take a look.

Be an Explorer

The best time to explore tide pools is during low tide or after a big storm, when the water level is lowest.

Here are some of the creatures you might discover.

CLAMS are soft-bodied animals with two round shells stuck together on one side like a hinge. If a clam finds itself threatened, it slams its shell closed to stay safe.

MUSSELS are like clams, but their shells are usually darker and not as round.

SEA ANEMONES (uh-NEHM-uh-neez) may look like beautiful plants, but don't be fooled. They are animals with long, swaying **tentacles**, or armlike structures. An anemone's tentacles have poisonous stingers that they use to catch their dinner.

CRABS are hard-shelled creatures that walk sideways on ten legs. They have claws that can pinch, so watch out!

PERIWINKLES are snails that feed on tiny plantlike creatures called **algae** (AL-jee). Algae can grow on tide pool rocks. Periwinkles are a popular snack for birds that live and hunt near the shore.

SEA URCHINS hang out at the bottom of tide pools. They are covered with long, sharp, poisonous spines, so don't touch!

Ready, Set, Explore!

Exploring a tide pool can be dangerous, so make sure an adult is around and follow these tips.

DO:

Walk carefully. Wet, algae-covered rocks can be slippery.

Research the tide schedule for the day so you can plan for the best time to see the pools.

Ask questions. There are many different kinds of creatures in tide pools. Be curious and talk about what you see.

Touch animals gently. Don't pry animals off rocks. Return anything you do move to the spot where you found it.

Take notes. Describe the animals you see. Take pictures or draw the creatures so that you'll remember them later.

DON'T:

Walk in tide pools. You can disturb or harm animals if you walk in tide pools. You could also hurt yourself on an animal's poisonous stinger or sharp spine.

Lose sight of the ocean. Big waves can catch you by surprise.

Take anything home. Starfish are pretty, but if you take one out of its pool, it will die. Leave the starfish in their homes when you go back to yours.

SEA STARS, or starfish, have hard, spiny skin. Most sea stars have five arms, but some have more. They use those arms to pry open the shells of clams and mussels.

RED ALGAE most often grow in salt water, where they attach themselves to rocks. Algae provide oxygen to underwater environments such as this tide pool.

Check In What are some of the rules for safely checking out tide pools? Why are these rules important?

Read to find out about the kinds of jobs people do on the North Atlantic coast.

Boats, Bogs, and Bolts

by Brett Gover

> Tourists float on Swan Boats in Boston's Public Garden. The boats have been a popular attraction since 1877.

For thousands of years, people have enjoyed living and working along the North Atlantic Ocean.

Native Americans first discovered the coast's rich soil, plentiful hunting grounds, and waters full of fish. In the 1600s, early settlers from Europe moved to start a new life in this land of plenty. It didn't take long for more settlers to join them. Fishing and farming villages sprung up in the area.

In less than 100 years, some of these coastal villages grew into towns. Some of the towns grew into cities such as Baltimore and Boston. As the populations grew, fishing and farming businesses also grew. Businesses built factories that needed more workers. Many people began leaving their small towns to work and live near the factories in larger communities.

Early factories made goods such as metal tools and **textiles**, or cloth. As time went on, the factories produced automobiles, submarines, plastics, and chemicals. The Atlantic Ocean's natural harbors made it a good place for shipping, or transporting goods by water. Huge ships carried many of these products to other places.

Today, tourism is another important industry along the North Atlantic coast. Millions of visitors come to see the bustling cities. This coast has a lot to offer visitors, including beaches, coastal scenery, boating trips, and historical sites.

Crabbing IN THE CHESAPEAKE BAY

On a summer afternoon, customers crowd a seafood market in Norfolk, Virginia. Many have come to buy blue crabs, displayed in glass tanks. Less than 12 hours ago, these shellfish were at the muddy bottom of Chesapeake Bay. How did they get to the market so quickly?

Joe, a local crab fisherman, could show you. Every morning, Joe and his crew rise before dawn and load their boat with the supplies, gear, and tools they need for a day of crabbing. They gather long poles with hooks on one end, wooden bushel baskets, rubber gloves, and a barrel full of bait.

Joe steers his boat out into the bay and soon reaches a line of colorful **buoys** (BOO-eez) stretching across the water. Each buoy is connected by a chain to a large wire trap called a crab pot at the bottom of the bay. Before they go crabbing, Joe's crew puts bait—stinky dead fish and worms—in each pot. When the crabs crawl into the pot to grab some of the bait, they get trapped. At each buoy, the crew snags the chain with the hooked pole, hauls up the pot, and dumps crabs onto a sorting table. The crabs are not happy, but the crew's gloves protect them from the crabs' pinching claws.

After putting fresh bait in each pot, Joe drops the pot back into the water. When he reaches the end of the line of buoys, he heads to another line, then another. By mid-afternoon, Joe and his crew have emptied the last of their 250 crab pots. Joe turns his boat toward the docks in Norfolk. Buyers will be happily waiting there for him.

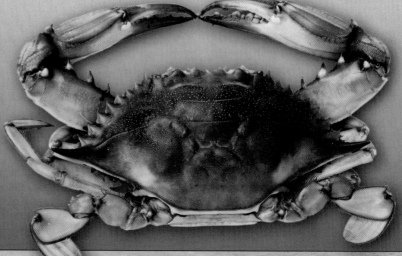

> Maryland blue crabs come from Chesapeake Bay. They get their name from the male crab's blue pinchers. The female blue crab has red pinchers. Both males and females are prized for their tasty meat.

A crab fisherman pulls a crab trap out of the water off the coast of Virginia Beach, Virginia.

Cranberry Farming IN MASSACHUSETTS

When you think of a farm, you might picture rolling fields, rows of crops, and red barns. You probably don't picture a mucky **bog**, or wet, spongy ground. It might surprise you to learn that one of the North Atlantic coast's top crops comes from bogs: cranberries!

Cranberries grow on vines rooted in a bog's spongy soil. The berries are green and tiny when they first appear, but they grow quickly. In the fall, as leaves change color, so do the berries. When the berries turn crimson red, they are ready for picking.

In southeastern Massachusetts, Belinda operates a cranberry farm that has been in her family for more than 75 years. In the farm's early days, the work was done mainly by hand. Today, it is done mostly by machine.

For most of her crop, Belinda uses a method called wet harvesting. Workers first flood the bog and then drive through it in big-wheeled vehicles that shake the berries from the vines. The berries float to the top of the water, where the workers use boards to corral them and push them onto a conveyor belt. The belt dumps them into a truck, which carries them to a processing plant to be made into sauces and juice. The next time you enjoy cranberry sauce, dried cranberries, or cranberry juice, you will know the journey the cranberries made.

> Workers gather cranberries floating in a flooded bog in Massachusetts.

The corralled cranberries are lifted by conveyer belt and then loaded into a truck. This worker is smoothing the piles on this almost full truck. Next stop for these cranberries will be the processing plant.

Shipyard Welding IN MAINE

Raul is average height, but at work he often feels tiny. You would too if you had his job. He helps build and repair enormous ships. Some of these ships stretch as long as two football fields. Raul is a welder at a shipyard in Maine.

Welding is a way of joining pieces of metal. A welder uses a tool called a welding torch. The welding torch produces intense heat. The heat allows the welder to melt two pieces of metal together, forming a strong bond. Raul usually spends his day welding together the large, rectangular plates of metal that form a ship's sides and bottom.

Welding is dangerous work. White-hot sparks shoot from the metal surfaces, and the noise can be deafening. Safety gear is very important. Raul wears heavy boots, leather gloves, and fire-resistant clothing, including a leather apron. Safety glasses and a helmet protect his eyes and face. Earplugs block much of the noise.

Maine has a long history of shipbuilding—it goes back more than 400 years! Skilled shipbuilders began moving to the coast of Maine for the work, helping to create a shipbuilding tradition there. Early shipbuilders took advantage of the dense forests near the coast to build their wooden ships. The forests provided many different kinds of wood needed for different parts of ships. But times have changed, and the ships are now mostly made of metal.

Building a ship can take years. When launch day finally arrives, Raul is filled with pride for the work that he has done.

The USS *Sir Winston Churchill* is a U.S. Navy ship built at the Bath Iron Works in Bath, Maine.

A welder uses his torch to repair the hull of a ship.

Check In Choose one of the jobs you read about and explain how that worker earns a living on the coast.

17

Lighting Up the Coastline

by David Holford

A ship is making a trip from Nova Scotia, Canada, to New York. It's having a rough journey. Howling winds, blinding rain, and rough seas fill the crew with fear. They can't see where they're going. Then, through the darkness, a light shines out into the sea. It shows where the land is and warns of rocks near the

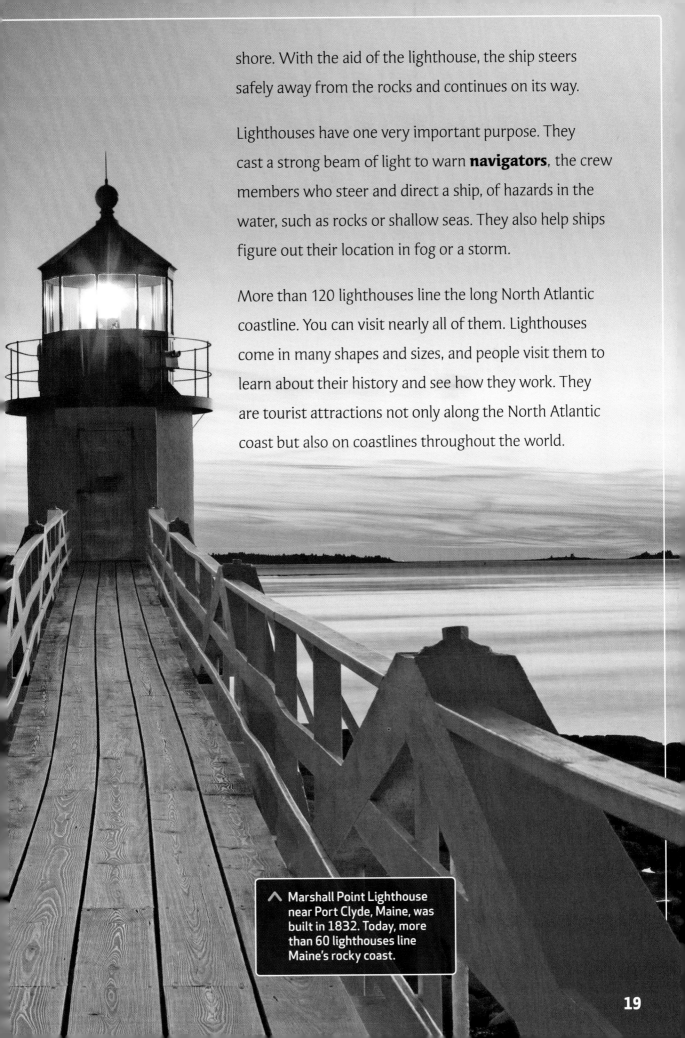

shore. With the aid of the lighthouse, the ship steers safely away from the rocks and continues on its way.

Lighthouses have one very important purpose. They cast a strong beam of light to warn **navigators**, the crew members who steer and direct a ship, of hazards in the water, such as rocks or shallow seas. They also help ships figure out their location in fog or a storm.

More than 120 lighthouses line the long North Atlantic coastline. You can visit nearly all of them. Lighthouses come in many shapes and sizes, and people visit them to learn about their history and see how they work. They are tourist attractions not only along the North Atlantic coast but also on coastlines throughout the world.

∧ Marshall Point Lighthouse near Port Clyde, Maine, was built in 1832. Today, more than 60 lighthouses line Maine's rocky coast.

Built to Last

The very first lighthouses in the United States were built in the early 1700s on the North Atlantic coast. Some very early lighthouses were made of wood, but most were simple round towers built from bricks or stone. Later, steel and concrete became the most common lighthouse building supplies. Stronger construction materials made it possible to build lighthouses offshore, directly in the water, and in a number of different shapes. But the tall, round tower is still common. It's what most people picture when they think of lighthouses.

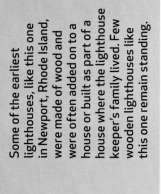

Some of the earliest lighthouses, like this one in Newport, Rhode Island, were made of wood and were often added on to a house or built as part of a house where the lighthouse keeper's family lived. Few wooden lighthouses like this one remain standing.

Cast-iron plate lighthouses are easier and cheaper to build than brick and stone lighthouses. They also need fewer repairs. Seen here, Cape Henry Lighthouse in Virginia is one of the tallest cast-iron lighthouses in the United States.

Stone lighthouses are made of concrete, brick, and other rock. These lighthouses are designed to be thicker at their base to support the stone's heavy weight. This is Old Cape Henry Lighthouse, and it is a historic landmark. It sits near the black-and-white lighthouse (at left) that is used today.

Skeletal lighthouses can be made of thin strips of iron and steel and have a column in the middle for the stairway. They use fewer materials and are very light. This design is often used for lighthouses built on sand or mud so that they won't sink. This lighthouse is in Marblehead, Massachusetts.

What's Inside?

Years ago, lighthouse keepers worked hard to keep ships safe. Today, most lighthouses are **automated**. Machines do work that used to be done by people. For example, a lighthouse keeper's main job used to be to light the lamp with a bright fire every night. Today, an electric light comes on every night automatically in most lighthouses. Modern lighthouses feature all sorts of cool technology, but many historic lighthouses have also been upgraded with modern conveniences, and they are a fusion of old and new. Read about some of the working parts of the Cape Cod, Massachusetts, lighthouse shown on this page.

At the top of the tower is the lantern room. It houses the light, or "lamp." The lamp needs to shine its light over a large area. To do this, it has a motor that turns the lamp when it is lit, so that the light seems to sweep across the surface of the ocean. Surrounding the outside of the lantern room is the catwalk. This narrow walkway allows the lantern room's windows to be easily cleaned.

A foghorn atop the lighthouse gives a loud blast every few seconds to warn ships during foggy conditions, when the light cannot be seen far offshore. On some lighthouses, antennas send out radio signals during fog and storms to alert ships on their radios.

Special lenses on the electric-powered lamp magnify its light. They also focus the light into a beam that can shine for more than 20 miles out to sea.

The tower raises the lantern room and lamp to a height that allows the lamp's beam to be seen from miles out at sea. Lighthouse towers must be strong enough to survive powerful storms and wind.

The round lantern room at the top of the tower has windows all around. This allows the light to shine in all directions, and it offers a great view of the coast and any ships that might pass by.

Some places have spiral staircases just because they are unusual and interesting looking. But in a tower like this lighthouse, it's the only kind of staircase that will even fit!

< Race Point Lighthouse, Cape Cod, Massachusetts

Unique and Unusual

You've learned about the most important features of lighthouses, and you've seen how they have changed over the years. Now check out these unique and unusual lighthouses—there are even some haunted ones!

Maine's West Quoddy Head Lighthouse lies at the farthest eastern point of the United States. You may have seen a picture of it before, because it appears on many calendars and travel posters.

Sheffield Island Lighthouse in Connecticut was built in 1868. It was a working lighthouse for 34 years, until 1902. Today it is a museum and is surrounded by a nature preserve.

The six-sided Drum Point Lighthouse originally stood in shallow waters off Maryland's coast. In 1975, the lighthouse was moved to stand outside a nearby museum.

Haunted Lighthouses

Cre-e-e-a-k . . . As you open the lighthouse door, something seems to push against it from the other side. After you enter, the door slams shut behind you. You feel someone's presence even though you're alone. What's going on? Could this lighthouse be haunted?

Point Lookout Lighthouse in Maryland is considered to be the most haunted lighthouse in the United States. Doors open and close for no reason. People hear voices, footsteps, and even snoring, but no one is there. Could captives from a prison camp for Civil War soldiers that once stood nearby be haunting the lighthouse?

Some people say Maine's Owls Head Light is home to the ghost of a former keeper. Many years ago, another keeper's three-year-old toddler woke her parents to warn, "Fog's rolling in! Time to put the foghorn on!" She explained that this information had come from her "imaginary friend," who looked like an old sea captain. Was this imaginary friend actually a ghost?

Check In How do lighthouses protect ships on the North Atlantic coast?

WHERE WILD PONIES RUN

by Elizabeth Massie

> The wild ponies of Assateague come in many colors. These include brown, black, tan, and spotted brown and white.

IN THE ORANGE LIGHT OF AN EARLY MORNING,

a herd of wild ponies gallops along the sandy beach. Heads and tails held high, the ponies run free. The pounding of their hooves sounds like soft thunder in the sand. They turn from the shore, race over the sand dunes to the grassy marshland, and then stop to graze. These are the wild ponies of Assateague (as-uh-TEEG) Island.

What's the difference between a horse and a pony? Ponies aren't young horses. They are smaller than other horses even when full grown.

Assateague is a long, narrow **barrier island** off the coast of Maryland and Virginia. The ponies have lived here, in the southernmost part of the North Atlantic coast region—and nowhere else—as far back as people can remember. But where did these ponies come from? No one knows for sure, but some local legends claim that they are **descendants**, or relatives, of ponies that swam to the island's shore when a Spanish ship wrecked off the coast around the year 1600.

On Assateague Island where the ponies live there is an area called a **refuge**—a place where wildlife is protected and can run free. The ponies roam the beaches, dunes, and marshes of the refuge without fences to stop them or stables to hold them. There are no people living on the island of Assateague. However, people do live on nearby Chincoteague (shing-kuh-TEEG) island.

Tourists visit Assateague Island to hike, canoe and kayak, and camp. However, the main reason they come is to see the ponies. The ponies bring in many tourists, which helps businesses in surrounding communities.

Thousands of people from around the world come each year to watch the ponies swim the channel between Assateague and Chincoteague Islands.

When the weather gets cold
the Assateague ponies grow
thick winter fur that helps
them stay warm.

THE PONY SWIM

There is only a certain amount of space for ponies on Assateague. To keep the island from becoming overcrowded, some of the young ponies are sold each year. Every summer, a town on Chincoteague Island holds an annual "pony swim" and carnival. This tradition has been held since 1925.

When it is time for the pony swim, cowboys gently round up the ponies on Assateague Island. Then they herd them into the **channel**, or narrow waterway, between Assateague and Chincoteague Islands. The people who herd the ponies to the sale are called saltwater cowboys. They always wait until the water in the channel is calm enough for the ponies to swim across safely. This time is called slack tide. The ponies are then paraded through the carnival grounds. The next day, after the young ponies are sold, the adult ponies swim back to Assateague Island where they run free again.

The citizens of the town made the sale a yearly event because both the town and the ponies benefitted from it. The sale generates money to improve the town, and the young ponies receive food and care. The carnival also helps the wild ponies that remain on Assateague. The sale keeps the number of wild ponies on the island under control.

KEEPING THE PONIES WILD

There is a downside to tourism on the island, though. When they are around humans a lot, wild ponies change their behavior. Some people in the community worry that the carnival events and the interaction with tourists are making the ponies tame, or less wild.

For instance, the ponies beg tourists for bags of potato chips and marshmallows. They are starting to prefer junk food to their regular food. Some ponies even trick the tourists into giving them the food. Adult ponies will nudge a baby pony in front of a slow-moving car full of tourists. When the driver of the car has to stop for the baby, the adult ponies gather at the sides of the car to beg for food.

Junk food is not good for the ponies, so park rangers enforce a rule that people cannot be within ten feet of the wild ponies. The rule is meant to stop people from feeding the ponies. Stopping the ponies' dependence on humans is one step in making sure the ponies remain wild.

These ponies have just crossed the channel to Chincoteague Island. The pony sale keeps the herd living on the island to about 160 ponies.

Many kinds of grasses grow on Assateague Island. The ponies eat grass, along with plants such as rosehips and bayberry twigs.

Check In How do the ponies of Assateague affect the lives of the people living on Chincoteague?

Discuss

1. What connections can you make among the five selections that you read in this book? How are the selections related?

2. Choose a feature of the North Atlantic coast that is most interesting to you or that you'd like to learn more about. Explain your choice.

3. What is one danger that tide pool creatures face at high tide? What is one danger they face at low tide?

4. Of the three jobs described in the selection "Boats, Bogs, and Bolts," which one would you least like to do? Explain your choice.

5. How could the popularity of the ponies on Assateague Island help or hurt them?